INSIDE MAJOR LEAGUE SOCCER

COLORADO RAPIDS

Katie Gillespie

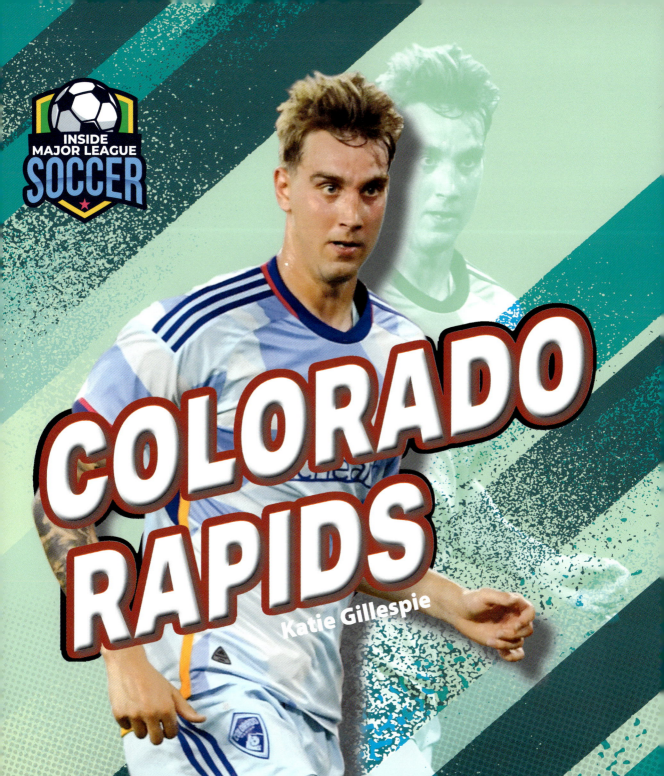

www.openlightbox.com

Step 1
Go to www.openlightbox.com

Step 2
Enter this unique code
AVG48653

Step 3
Explore your interactive eBook!

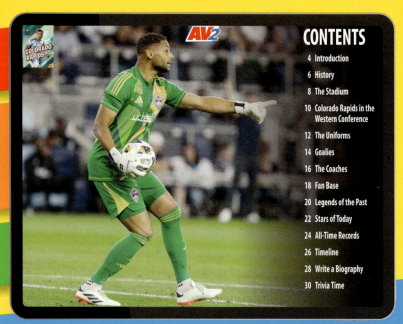

AV2 is optimized for use on any device

Your interactive eBook comes with...

Contents
Browse a live contents page to easily navigate through resources

Audio
Listen to sections of the book read aloud

Videos
Watch informative video clips

Weblinks
Gain additional information for research

Slideshows
View images and captions

Try This!
Complete activities and hands-on experiments

Key Words
Study vocabulary, and complete a matching word activity

Quizzes
Test your knowledge

Share
Share titles within your Learning Management System (LMS) or Library Circulation System

Citation
Create bibliographical references following APA, CMOS, and MLA styles

This title is part of our AV2 digital subscription

1-Year Grades K–5 Subscription
ISBN 978-1-7911-3320-7

Access hundreds of AV2 titles with our digital subscription.
Sign up for a FREE trial at www.openlightbox.com/trial

The digital components of this book are guaranteed to stay active for at least five years from the date of publication.

COLORADO RAPIDS

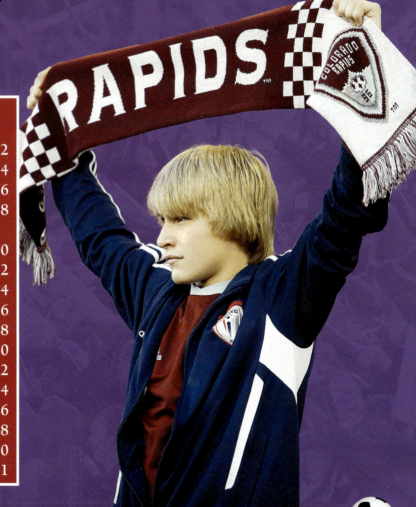

CONTENTS

Interactive eBook Code 2
Introduction 4
History. 6
The Stadium 8
Colorado Rapids in the
    Western Conference 10
The Uniforms 12
Goalies. 14
The Coaches 16
Fan Base 18
Legends of the Past 20
Stars of Today 22
All-Time Records 24
Timeline 26
Write a Biography 28
Trivia Time 30
Key Words/Index. 31

Introduction

Denver, the state capital of Colorado, is located near the Rocky Mountains. It has an **elevation** of 1 mile (1.6 kilometers). This is why Denver is nicknamed the "Mile High City."

There are many professional sports teams in Denver. Among these is the city's Major League Soccer (MLS) team, the Colorado Rapids. The Rapids are based in Commerce City, Colorado, which is part of the Denver **metropolitan area**.

MLS was formed in 1995, with its first season of play occurring in 1996. At the time, there were only 10 **clubs** in the league. Since then, the number of teams has tripled to 30. The league is divided into the Eastern Conference and the Western Conference. Each has 15 members. The Colorado Rapids belong to the Western Conference.

Midfielder Djordje Mihailovic joined the Rapids in 2024. His transfer fee was reportedly more than $3 million, making it a club record.

Stadium	DICK'S Sporting Goods Park	**Location**	Commerce City, Colorado, United States
Conference	Western Conference, Major League Soccer	**Championships**	MLS Cup (2010)
Head Coach	Chris Armas	**Nicknames**	'Pids, Burgundy & Blue, Boys in Burgundy, Burgundy Boys

INSIDE MAJOR LEAGUE SOCCER

1996

The Colorado Rapids named midfielder Chris Henderson their **first-ever Most Valuable Player (MVP)** in 1996.

$131 MILLION

DICK'S Sporting Goods Park cost a total of **$131 million** to build.

8

Commerce City is about **7 miles (11 kilometers)** north of downtown Denver.

COLORADO RAPIDS 5

History

The Colorado Rapids were first established in October 1995 as one of the original 10 MLS clubs. Their name comes from Colorado's fast-moving rivers. Although they finished last in the Western Conference in their first season, the Rapids found success the following year, making it all the way to the MLS Cup Final. They lost the championship to D.C. United but started to amass a dedicated fan base. Colorado made the playoffs again for the next three years, although they never went further than the conference semifinals.

After missing the playoffs in 2001, the Rapids made it to the conference finals in 2002. They continued to make the playoffs each year, until a turning point came in 2007 with the club's move from Denver to Commerce City. The Rapids failed to qualify for the playoffs three seasons in a row after their move. However, they made a triumphant return in 2010. That year, the Rapids reached the finals, defeating FC Dallas and winning the MLS Cup.

After this historic win, Colorado struggled. The Rapids missed the playoffs six more times. However, hopes remained high, and Colorado made the conference semifinals in 2021. They missed the playoffs again in 2022 and 2023, but finally qualified in 2024, under the direction of new head coach Chris Armas. The club's fans have high expectations in the future for this beloved franchise.

Before winning the MLS Cup, the Rapids reached the conference finals in both 2005 and 2006.

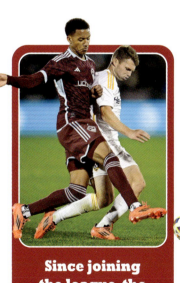

Since joining the league, the Colorado Rapids have qualified for the MLS playoffs a total of 16 times.

The Stadium

When the Rapids first joined MLS in 1996, they played their home matches at Mile High Stadium in Denver. The Rapids remained at Mile High until the end of 2001. It closed shortly after and was demolished the following year. To replace Mile High Stadium, a new venue was built. It was initially called Invesco Field at Mile High. The Rapids moved into the stadium in 2002 and stayed until 2006. Renamed multiple times over the years, the venue is known as Empower Field at Mile High today. It is currently home to the Denver Broncos of the National Football League (NFL).

In 2004, a new stadium project was announced in nearby Commerce City. Ground broke on September 28, 2005, and the venue officially opened on April 7, 2007. After sharing with the Broncos for 11 seasons, the Rapids finally had a home stadium of their own. Called DICK'S Sporting Goods Park, this soccer-specific venue is part of a complex that also includes youth soccer **pitches**, retail establishments, and a civic center.

The first match at DICK'S Sporting Goods Park was between the Colorado Rapids and D.C. United.

DICK'S Sporting Goods Park seats about 18,000 people for sporting events. This expands to 27,000 for concerts and festivals.

COLORADO RAPIDS

Colorado Rapids in the Western Conference

WESTERN CONFERENCE

1. Austin FC
2. Colorado Rapids
3. FC Dallas
4. Houston Dynamo FC
5. LA Galaxy
6. Los Angeles FC
7. Minnesota United FC
8. Portland Timbers
9. Real Salt Lake
10. San Diego FC
11. San Jose Earthquakes
12. Seattle Sounders FC
13. Sporting Kansas City
14. St. Louis City SC
15. Vancouver Whitecaps FC

EASTERN CONFERENCE

- Atlanta United FC
- CF Montréal
- Charlotte FC
- Chicago Fire FC
- Columbus Crew
- D.C. United
- FC Cincinnati
- Inter Miami CF
- Nashville SC
- New England Revolution
- New York City FC
- New York Red Bulls
- Orlando City SC
- Philadelphia Union
- Toronto FC

INSIDE MAJOR LEAGUE SOCCER

Colorado Rapids vs FC Dallas

On November 21, 2010, at BMO Field in Toronto, Canada, the Rapids faced off against FC Dallas in the MLS Cup Final. Things were looking dire for Colorado in the first half of the game. Dallas midfielder and league MVP David Ferreira scored the first goal of the match in minute 35. Although they were down 1–0, the Rapids persisted, with forward Conor Casey tying the match in minute 57. With the score equalized, the game went into overtime. Finally, in minute 107, Colorado forward Macoumba Kandji made a cross that deflected off Dallas **defender** George John and found the back of the net. The goal meant the Rapids brought home the 2010 MLS Cup, their first major trophy in franchise history.

The logo on the Rapids' away jersey is circular, with a red letter "C" around a soccer ball.

The Uniforms

The primary colors of the Colorado Rapids are claret and sky blue, with white, silver, and onyx as additional colors. The team's current home uniforms are called the One Flag Kit. Used in 2024 and 2025, the jerseys are mostly burgundy with a waved checker pattern. Accents in sky blue can be found on the neck and sleeves. **Logos** are found on the chest.

A new away kit was introduced in February 2025. It will be worn for both the 2025 and 2026 seasons. Known as the Headwaters Kit, it was inspired by the flowing rivers of the Rocky Mountains and other Colorado waterways. The jerseys are a combination of light mint green and dark green. The team's secondary logo appears on the chest for the first time in franchise history.

Since 2007, the team's main logo has been a shield in burgundy and blue. "Colorado Rapids" is written in white on a burgundy background. A mountain range sits below this, with a soccer ball in the middle. The number 96 is at the bottom, a reference to the year the club joined the MLS.

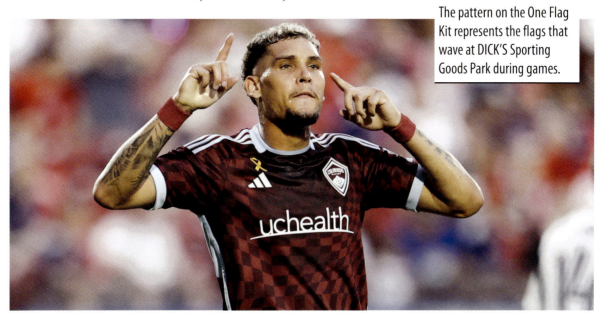

The pattern on the One Flag Kit represents the flags that wave at DICK'S Sporting Goods Park during games.

Goalies

Each team's **goalkeeper** wears a unique uniform. It often features long sleeves, pants, and extra padding in order to provide additional protection. Goalie jerseys usually come in vibrant colors. This makes them stand out from other players and match officials so that they are easy to identify at a glance.

During his short time as the team's primary goalkeeper, Zack Steffen has already found great success as one of the club's top-rated players. He started his professional soccer career in Germany in 2015. Steffen joined MLS in 2016, playing for the Columbus Crew. He joined the Colorado Rapids in 2024, making 33 appearances and starts. Steffen won the club's Defensive Player of the Year and Humanitarian of the Year awards. He also earned a nomination for 2024 MLS Goalkeeper of the Year and was runner-up for Newcomer of the Year at the Colorado Rapids Press Corps Awards.

Goalies typically wear gloves, allowing for maximum grip when handling the ball.

In 2024, Zack Steffen recorded six clean sheets, or games in which he did not allow a single goal.

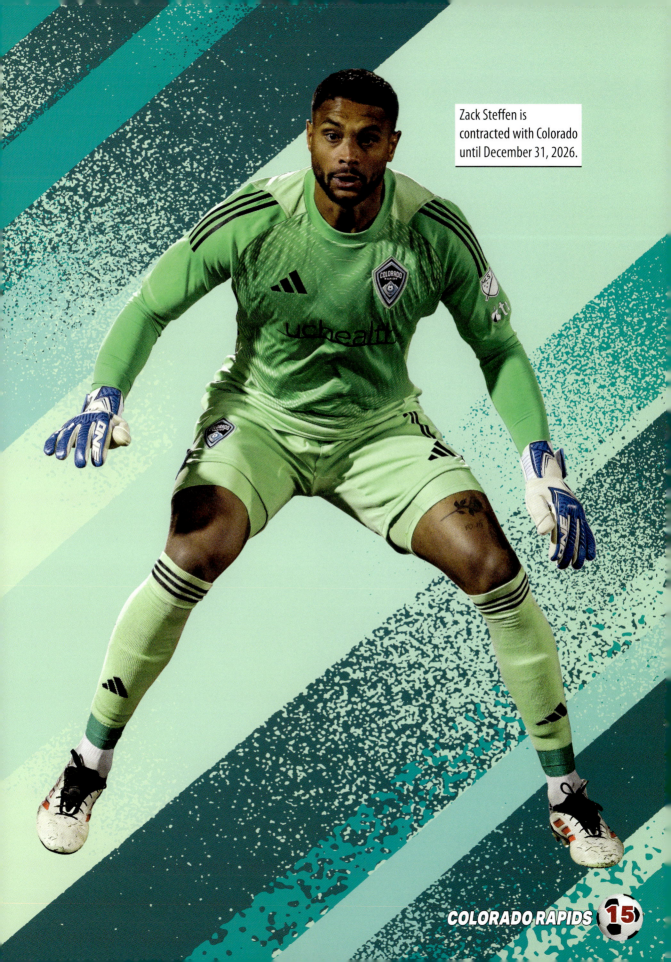

Chris Armas was inducted into the National Soccer Hall of Fame in May 2025.

The Coaches

Since Colorado's inaugural MLS season in 1996, there have been 10 full-time head coaches. Each has impacted the club and its legacy in his own way. However, some have played more important roles in the club's story than others.

GLENN MYERNICK Glenn Myernick started coaching the Rapids during their first MLS season. He served as the team's second full-time head coach, taking over from Bob Houghton in November 1996. Myernick was in charge of the club when they made it all the way to the MLS Cup finals against D.C. United in 1997. He still holds the record for most matches of any head coach in franchise history, with 145. Myernick passed away in 2010 and was inducted into the National Soccer Hall of Fame in 2015.

GARY SMITH English coach Gary Smith is widely considered to be one of the top coaches that Colorado has ever had. He began serving as an assistant coach for the club in February 2008. Smith took on the position of interim head coach later that year, and he was officially appointed as manager in November 2008. He is perhaps best known for bringing the Rapids to victory in the 2010 MLS Cup final, which was team's first major trophy and biggest win to date. Smith left Colorado in 2011.

CHRIS ARMAS Chris Armas is a former defensive midfielder who was the U.S. Soccer Male Athlete of the Year in 2000. During his playing career, he also won an MLS Cup, a Supporters' Shield, and four Lamar Hunt U.S. Open Cups with the Chicago Fire. He is Colorado's current head coach, having joined the club on November 17, 2023. Armas is already one of the team's most successful managers. In 2024, he led the Rapids to the playoffs for the first time since 2021 and set several club records. His exceptional performance earned Armas the 2024 Colorado Rapids Press Corps Award for Story of the Year.

Fan Base

In 2013, three of Colorado's independent supporter groups came together to form a new group. The Bulldogs Supporters Group, Pid Army, and Class 6 merged into Centennial 38. The name pays tribute to the fact that Colorado became the 38th state during America's centennial year. Centennial 38 collaborated with the Rapids in February 2025 to introduce the South Bank, a section specifically for supporters.

Colorado has had multiple mascots over the years. The first was RapidMan, who was introduced for the team's inaugural 1996 season. He was replaced by Edson the Eagle, a bald eagle who represented the team's courage, freedom, and spirit. Soon after, Edson was joined by Marco Van Bison, followed by a raccoon named Jorge El Mapache. Franz the Fox came next, rounding out the quartet of animal mascots.

FAN FACTS

1. RapidMan made a triumphant return in 2020, ahead of Colorado's 25th MLS season.

2. Rapids fans can stay up to date with the team online. The club has more than 550,000 followers across their social media platforms.

Found on the south endline at DICK'S Sporting Goods Park, the South Bank helps unite the team's most passionate fans as they chant, sing, and cheer the Rapids on to victory.

INSIDE MAJOR LEAGUE SOCCER

Legends of the Past

Over the years, plenty of exceptional players have called Colorado home. Although many of them are no longer with the club, they have helped shape it. These league legends are some of the best ever to suit up for the Rapids.

MARCELO BALBOA

Marcelo Balboa played for the Rapids during the team's first six MLS seasons. A true star from the beginning, he notched the first goal in franchise history and contributed two out of three goals to the club's first win. During Balboa's time with Colorado, the club made the playoffs on four consecutive occasions, from 1997 to 2000. He also earned five consecutive All-Star selections while with the Rapids, from 1997 to 2001. In May 2001, Balboa set a league record as the first defender to tally more than 20 goals and 20 **assists**. In total, he made 146 starts in 151 appearances for the club, scoring 24 goals and making 12 assists. Not only is Balboa one of the greatest members the franchise has ever seen, he is often considered among the top players in the league. In 2003, he became the first inductee into the Rapids Gallery of Honor, along with Paul Bravo. Balboa was inducted into the National Soccer Hall of Fame in 2005.

Position: Defender
Years in Pro Soccer: 1987–2002, 1996–2001 for Colorado
Born: August 8, 1967, Chicago, Illinois, United States

PABLO MASTROENI

Pablo Mastroeni joined Colorado in 2002. He became team captain in September 2004, a position he held throughout the rest of his tenure with the club. Mastroeni was named an MLS All-Star a total of nine consecutive times, which tied him for second-most in the league. Of his All-Star appearances, seven were as a Rapid, from 2002 to 2008. The most decorated player in franchise history, Mastroeni also earned three club MVP awards, in 2007, 2008, and 2010. He was instrumental in Colorado's 2010 MLS Cup victory. In August 2011, Mastroeni became just the third MLS player ever to start 300 regular season games. He retired from playing in 2013. Then, he became head coach of the Rapids in 2014, the same year he was inducted into the club's Gallery of Honor. Mastroeni left the franchise in 2017. His number 25 was retired in 2021. It was the first number ever to be retired by Colorado.

Position: Defender
Years in Pro Soccer: 1998–2013, 2002–2013 for Colorado
Born: August 29, 1976, Mendoza, Argentina

CONOR CASEY

Conor Casey joined the Rapids in 2007 and was named the club's Comeback Player of the Year that season. Although he missed the first nine games of 2008 due to injury, Casey still led the club in goals that year, with 11. Among them was a hat trick that included a 90th-minute match-winning goal. Casey was the team's top scorer again in 2009, racking up 16 goals and setting a franchise record. He was crucial to the club's victory in the 2010 MLS Cup, scoring the equalizing goal of the final. This earned him the match's MVP award. Over the course of his time with the Rapids, Casey made 119 appearances before leaving the team at the end of 2012. Not only is Casey well known among Rapids fans, he is one of the most celebrated strikers in the league. Casey retired as a player after the 2016 season. He later returned to Colorado in 2017 as an assistant coach, the same year he was inducted into the club's Gallery of Honor. Casey served as the Rapids' interim manager from May to August 2019.

Position: Forward
Years in Pro Soccer: 2000–2016, 2007–2012 for Colorado
Born: July 25, 1981, Dover, New Hampshire, United States

Stars of Today

The Colorado Rapids are stacked with impressive talent. Among these skilled players are some up-and-coming stars. Here are a few of the most outstanding athletes on the team's current roster.

COLE BASSETT

Cole Bassett joined the Colorado Rapids **Academy** in 2017. The following year, he was signed to the Rapids as a **homegrown player**. He made his MLS debut on September 8, 2018, as the youngest player in franchise history at the time. Bassett's breakout season in 2020 saw him become the club's top scorer, with five goals. He scored another five in 2021. Bassett led Colorado in goals once again in 2023, with six. He ended the 2024 season with nine goals and seven assists, both career highs. Bassett was named runner-up Player of the Year, and his three goals in the Rocky Mountain Cup were recognized in the Goal of the Year category. In January 2025, his younger brother Sam signed with Colorado as well, making them the club's first pair of homegrown brothers.

Position: Midfielder
Years in Pro Soccer: 2018–present, joined Colorado in 2018
Born: July 28, 2001, Littleton, Colorado, United States

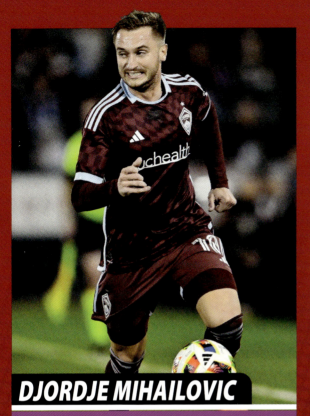

DJORDJE MIHAILOVIC

Djordje Mihailovic joined the MLS in 2017 as a homegrown player for the Chicago Fire. After playing for several teams, including Dutch club Alkmaar Zaanstreek for the 2023 season, he returned to the United States in 2024 to play for the Colorado Rapids. Although he has only been with the Rapids for a short time, Mihailovic has already proven himself to be indispensable. In 2024, he set a franchise record of 21 for goal contributions, including 10 assists and a career-best 11 goals. This performance led Mihailovic to win the club's MVP and Players' Player of the Year awards. The Colorado Rapids Press Corps named him both the 2024 Player of the Year and Newcomer of the Year. He was recognized in the Goal of the Year and Stat of the Year categories as well. Mihailovic is contracted with the Rapids until December 2027, with an option for 2028.

Position: Midfielder
Years in Pro Soccer: 2017–present, joined Colorado in 2024
Born: November 10, 1998, Jacksonville, Florida, United States

RAFAEL NAVARRO

Rafael Navarro started playing soccer professionally in 2020, in his native Brazil. He was a member of Botafogo de Futebol e Regatas, making a total of 63 appearances, 18 goals, and 10 assists for the club. Next, Navarro joined Sociedade Esportiva Palmeiras in 2022 and helped them win the league title. He was loaned out from Palmeiras to the Colorado Rapids in July 2023. That season, he played in 10 matches, recording a goal and an assist. In 2024, Navarro had a breakout season. He became Colorado's top scorer, notching 15 goals. This earned him a nomination for the 2024 MLS MVP award. Navarro was also recognized by the Colorado Rapids Press Corps in the category of Goal of the Year. Navarro signed a permanent deal with the Rapids in June 2024, keeping him in Colorado through the end of 2027, with an option for 2028.

Position: Forward
Years in Pro Soccer: 2020–present, joined Colorado in 2023
Born: April 14, 2000, Cabo Frio, Brazil

All-Time Records

225
Appearances
Pablo Mastroeni holds the club record for most appearances, with 225. He also leads the Rapids in matches started, with 217, and minutes played, with 18,669.

61,000+
Highest Attendance
On July 4, 2002, the Rapids defeated the Chicago Fire 3–2 in a home game at Invesco Field at Mile High. The match set a club record for attendance, with more than 61,000 fans in the crowd.

53
Most Assists
With a total of 53, Chris Henderson holds the franchise record for most assists. He also leads the club in shots, with 342, and shots on goal, with 151.

INSIDE MAJOR LEAGUE SOCCER

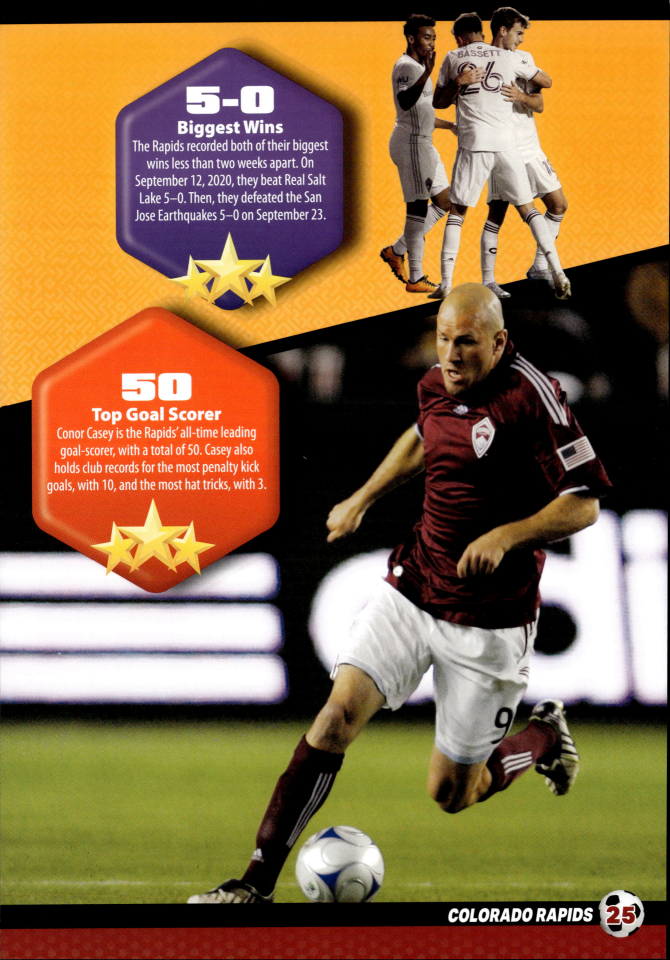

5-0
Biggest Wins
The Rapids recorded both of their biggest wins less than two weeks apart. On September 12, 2020, they beat Real Salt Lake 5–0. Then, they defeated the San Jose Earthquakes 5–0 on September 23.

50
Top Goal Scorer
Conor Casey is the Rapids' all-time leading goal-scorer, with a total of 50. Casey also holds club records for the most penalty kick goals, with 10, and the most hat tricks, with 3.

Timeline

As one of the original MLS teams, the Colorado Rapids have a long history in the league. Across nearly three decades of play, the club has been through its share of both highs and lows. Here are some of the franchise's biggest moments.

1996
The Rapids play their first MLS season. Chris Henderson is named the club's first MVP.

2007
The Rapids move from Denver to Commerce City, with the opening of DICK'S Sporting Goods Park in April.

2002
The Rapids move from Mile High Stadium to the newly built Invesco Field at Mile High.

1995
The Colorado Rapids join MLS as one of the league's founding members.

1997
Colorado makes it to the finals of the MLS playoffs, ending the season as runners-up for the MLS Cup.

2005
In September, ground breaks on DICK'S Sporting Goods Park, Colorado's new soccer-specific venue.

26 INSIDE MAJOR LEAGUE SOCCER

2010
Colorado defeats FC Dallas 2–1 in the MLS Cup final, earning the franchise's first major trophy.

2020
In honor of the team's 25th MLS season, RapidMan returns. In September, Colorado has two 5–0 wins, their biggest in franchise history.

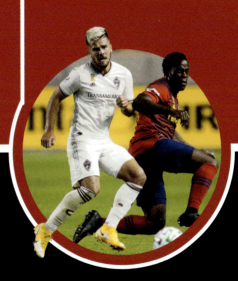

2013
The Bulldogs Supporters Group, Pid Army, and Class 6 come together to form Centennial 38, Colorado's largest supporters' group.

The Future
With new players such as Djordje Mihailovic, who set the club record for goal contributions in 2024, and new head coach Chris Armas, who led Colorado to the playoffs for the first time in three seasons, hopes for the future are high.

Write a Biography

Life Story
A person's life story can be the subject of a book. This kind of book is called a biography. Biographies often describe the lives of people who have achieved great success. These people may be alive today, or they may have lived many years ago. Reading a biography can help you learn more about a great person.

Get the Facts
Use this book, and research in the library and on the internet, to find out more about your favorite Colorado Rapids player or coach. Learn as much about this person as you can. What are this person's statistics in important categories? Has this person set any records? Also, be sure to write down key events in the person's life. What was the player or coach's childhood like? What has this person accomplished off the field? Is there anything else that makes this person special or unusual?

Use the Concept Web
A concept web is a useful research tool. Read the questions in the concept web on the following page. Answer the questions in your notebook. Your answers will help you write a biography.

INSIDE MAJOR LEAGUE SOCCER

Concept Web

Adulthood
- Where does this individual currently reside?
- Does this person have a family?

Your Opinion
- What did you learn from the sources you used in your research?
- Would you suggest these sources to others?
- Was anything missing from these sources?

Childhood
- Where and when was this person born?
- Describe this person's parents, siblings, and friends.
- Did this person grow up in unusual circumstances?

Accomplishments off the Field
- What is this person's life's work?
- Has this person received awards or recognition for accomplishments?
- How have this person's accomplishments served others?

Writing the Biography

Help and Obstacles
- Did this individual have a positive attitude?
- Did this person receive help from others?
- Did this person have a mentor?
- Did this person face any hardships?
- If so, how were the hardships overcome?

Accomplishments on the Field
- What records does this person hold?
- What key games and plays have defined this person's career?
- What are this individual's stats in categories important to this individual's position?

Work and Preparation
- What was this person's education?
- What was this person's work experience?
- How does this person work?
- What is the process this person uses?

Trivia Time

Take this quiz to test your knowledge of the Colorado Rapids. The answers are printed upside down under each question.

1. Who scored the tying goal in Colorado's MLS Cup win?
A. Conor Casey

2. How many assists does Chris Henderson have?
A. 53

3. Who are the Rapids' four animal mascots?
A. Edson the Eagle, Marco Von Bison, Jorge El Mapache, and Franz the Fox

4. In what year did the Rapids win the MLS Cup?
A. 2010

5. Which former head coach holds the franchise record for most matches?
A. Glenn Myernick

6. Where is DICK'S Sporting Goods Park?
A. Commerce City, Colorado

7. What is Colorado's new away kit called?
A. The Headwaters Kit

8. What was the Rapids' first home venue?
A. Mile High Stadium

9. Who was Colorado's top scorer in 2024?
A. Rafael Navarro

10. Why is Denver nicknamed the "Mile High City?"
A. It has an elevation of 1 mile (1.6 km)

11. Who won Colorado's Defensive Player of the Year award in 2024?
A. Zack Steffen

12. What record did Marcelo Balboa set in May 2001?
A. The first defender ever to tally more than 20 goals and 20 assists

30 **INSIDE MAJOR LEAGUE SOCCER**

Key Words

academy: a place where people train in a special field

assists: passes that lead directly to a goal

clubs: groups focused on a particular interest or activity

defender: a player on a soccer team whose job it is to stop opponents from scoring

elevation: distance above sea level

goalkeeper: also called a goalie, the player responsible for keeping the ball from going into the goal and the only player who is allowed to pick up the ball

homegrown player: a player signed directly to a team from its own academy program

logos: symbols made up of text and images that identify a team

metropolitan area: a city and its surrounding area

pitches: areas that are used for playing sports

Index

Armas, Chris 4, 7, 16, 17, 27

Balboa, Marcelo 20, 30
Bassett, Cole 22
Bassett, Sam 22
Bravo, Paul 20

Casey, Conor 11, 21, 25, 30
Centennial 38 12, 18, 27
Commerce City 4, 5, 7, 8, 26, 30

DICK'S Sporting Goods Park 4, 5, 8, 9, 13, 18, 26, 30

Edson the Eagle 18, 30

Franz the Fox 18, 30

Gallery of Honor 20, 21

Headwaters Kit 13, 30
Henderson, Chris 5, 24, 26, 30

Invesco Field at Mile High 8, 24, 26

Jorge El Mapache 18, 30

Kandji, Macoumba 11

Marco Van Bison 18, 30
Mastroeni, Pablo 21, 24
Mihailovic, Djordje 4, 23, 27
Mile High Stadium 8, 26, 30
MLS Cup 4, 7, 11, 17, 21, 26, 27, 30
Myernick, Glenn 17, 30

National Soccer Hall of Fame 16, 17, 20
Navarro, Rafael 23, 30

One Flag Kit 13

RapidMan 18, 27

Smith, Gary 17
South Bank 18
Steffen, Zack 14, 15, 30

Get the best of both worlds.

AV2 bridges the gap between print and digital.

The expandable resources toolbar enables quick access to content including **videos**, **audio**, **activities**, **weblinks**, **slideshows**, **quizzes**, and **key words**.

Animated videos make static images come alive.

Resource icons on each page help readers to further **explore key concepts**.

Published by Lightbox Learning Inc.
276 5th Avenue, Suite 704 #917
New York, NY 10001
Website: www.openlightbox.com

Copyright ©2026 Lightbox Learning Inc.
All rights reserved. No part of this publication may be reproduced, stored in a retrieval system, or transmitted in any form or by any means, electronic, mechanical, photocopying, recording, or otherwise, without the prior written permission of the publisher.

Library of Congress Cataloging-in-Publication Data

Names: Gillespie, Katie author
Title: Colorado Rapids / Katie Gillespie.
Description: New York, NY : Lightbox Learning Inc, 2026. | Series: Inside Major League Soccer | Includes index. | Audience: Grades 4-6
Identifiers: LCCN 2025013693 (print) | LCCN 2025013694 (ebook) | ISBN 9798874525897 library binding | ISBN 9798874525910 ebook other | ISBN 9798874525934 ebook other
Subjects: LCSH: Colorado Rapids (Soccer team)--Juvenile literature
Classification: LCC GV943.6.C585 G55 2026 (print) | LCC GV943.6.C585 (ebook) | DDC 796.334/630978883--dc23/eng/20250512
LC record available at https://lccn.loc.gov/2025013693
LC ebook record available at https://lccn.loc.gov/2025013694

Printed in Fargo, North Dakota, in the United States of America
1 2 3 4 5 6 7 8 9 0   29 28 27 26 25

072025
101324

Project Coordinator John Willis
Art Director Terry Paulhus
Layout Jean Faye Rodriguez

Photo Credits
The publisher has made every reasonable effort to trace ownership and to obtain permission to use copyright material. The publisher would be pleased to have any errors or omissions brought to its attention so that they may be corrected in subsequent printings. Some visual elements in this title may have been generated using AI. While we strive for accuracy in all aspects of our products, we cannot guarantee that the elements depicted in these images are accurate. The publisher acknowledges Getty Images, Alamy, Shutterstock, and Wikimedia as the primary image suppliers for this title.

If you have any inquiries about these images or would like to provide any feedback, please reach out to us at feedback@openlightbox.com. All of the Internet URLs and Google Maps links given in the interactive eBook were valid at the time of publication. However, due to the dynamic nature of the Internet, some addresses may have changed, or sites may have ceased to exist since publication. While the author and publisher regret any inconvenience this may cause readers, no responsibility for any such changes can be accepted by either the author or the publisher.

View new titles and product videos at www.openlightbox.com